Walpurgis Night

joan cofrancesco

authorHOUSE®

AuthorHouse™
1663 Liberty Drive
Bloomington, IN 47403
www.authorhouse.com
Phone: 1 (800) 839-8640

Cover Art by Janine Bartolotti

Published by AuthorHouse 12/05/2017

ISBN: 978-1-5462-1989-7 (sc)
ISBN: 978-1-5462-1988-0 (e)

Print information available on the last page.

This book is printed on acid-free paper.

Preface

Walpurgis Night or Walpurgisnacht Night May Eve, April 30, has traditionally been regarded as a night when dark forces are afoot. In Germany, Walpurgis Night is associated with Mt. Brocken in the Herz ranges, for it was here that the witches were said to gather and hold their sabbath. It was believed to be a night of witch revelry throughout Germany, the Low Countries, and Scandanavia. Witches mounted their brooms and flew to mountaintops, where they carried on with wild feasting, dancing and copulation with Demons.

May Eve was also a time of "wearing of the green" in honor of Earth's new green garment, as well as a time of sexual license, symbolizing nature's fertilization: a honeymoon when marriage bonds were temporarily forgotten and sexual freedom prevailed in rural districts until the 16th century.

THIS BOOK IS DEDICATED TO

JANINE

Walpurgis Night
    (after Adrienne Rich)

Ten AM and I am still here
Amazing
Poems, carbons, journals scattered everywhere
brandy spilt on the desk
cold coffee beside the typewriter
No one exists in this study
without first confronting the demons
the photos of dead poets—
Sylvia Plath, Anne Sexton
the spirit of the writer who died
prematurely in this room
the ghost of the muse
who walked out years ago
I feel driven
What demon is turning my life
into one long poem?

9-Lives

I've been after the East
For years: Kabir
and Snyder on my shelves
exotic incense in the air
sitting on my oriental rug
in the Lotus position.
I'm sick of the dog-food mentality
of the West
I'm sick of our obsession
with things
My siamese cat licks me.
Even he likes tofu.

Sestina On Six Words By Anne Sexton

I woke by my woodstove
with *45 Mercy Street*
still in my hand, still feeling the Fury
of the fire above my head
thinking of you and the others
who worshipped God and Death.

What did you want from Death?
Once you put your head in the stove
did you expect Him to treat you different from the others?
Did you think he would come down your street
pull out your head
and say I understood your Fury?

And what have you gained by your Fury?
Death?
and one less voice in my head
one less book above my stove
one less late light burning on my street
one less person hearing the tin drum of THE OTHER.

Yesterday was a day like no other
I experienced Fury
Oh, how the street
toward Death
did leap and the brightness from my stove
fell down and rippled the bricks above my head

But I did not let it go to my head
like you and Sylvia and the others
who found it easier to face the stove
than face the challenge of writing more Fury
poems about Death
and Fairy tales told once in awhile on the street.

I saw God dressed up like an old man on the street
staggering out of His shoes, talking out of his head
and I thought about Death
And others, others, others
And Ms Dog I thought about Fury
but unlike you I went home to cook on my stove.

There is no way to ease my head or the head of others.
Your street leads only to Death—
A land of stoves and Fury.

Anne In the Prison Of Her Own Kitchen

anne peers into the wilderness and hears the faucets driving
like storms on white porcelain.
she scrubs the oven grease from her chin and whips
the cobwebs from her hair.
bars soften on her sink and the light from her window
mellows on the mops that never dried.
anne goes from object to object, from dish to asphalt tile,
from spoon to chipped glass.
while her stomach aches with housewives' blight and clouds
and busted appliances dangle and smear across her mind
she sags and watches her face leap in the ripples of her
reflection and now she suffers, she suffers.
her kitchen tells her days. it is the place where she drains
her hair oil into swirling rains. it is the place
where she subdues her sorrows and lets her gums
bleed with a taste like rusty Drano cans.

Christmas Eve Poem

3 in the morning.
My eyes full of Christmas Night
Maddipal incense.
I eat plums and pomegranates
in bed
with my lover
The cat staying in the warm
blue sheets.
We shall open our presents.

Field of Dreams

Sylvia Plath writes about
horses and belljars
with a Cheshire cat grin
Anne Sexton writes about
Spoons and God
stoned on thorazine
Gertrude Stein writes about
Alice B.
high on hash brownies.
Ladies,
today I write to you—
a B-rated poet thinking
If I hallucinated about dead
rats in the toilet
If I raged naked
at the night
If I died
in my mother's fur...
Perhaps one day
we would meet
for drinks on the deck
of a bar in Provincetown
on a sweaty August noon
to discuss lovers and
Spoons.

Madame Blavatsky

Madame Blavatsky is back again. I
saw her grand form romping through
the Russian Tea Room,
drooling over Moscow mules,
searching for Barishnikov
and Nureyev.

Madame Blavatsky is back again. I
caught her last night dancing
at the Red Parrot Disco
and then at a video shop
renting Dr. Zhivago.
The salesgirl never considered
charging her being
the only Russian icon in the 20th Century.

Pap Smear

I mount your examining table
push my feet into stirrups—
you in your starched white jacket
adjust your miner's light
stare into labyrinths of lips   heavy breathing
smooth on sterile flexam latex gloves
shove in thick tongs   spread them
doctor take it easy
I look upside down at your framed diploma
You look at my vagina
neither licks nor caresses
                                        only
probes of stainless steel.

Our Life Is Our Art

Sometimes you talk as if Lennon
were still alive.
His photo taped to your refrigerator
Shaved Fish coming out of your speakers.
It is a cold December in Syracuse
I sit by the fire reading Tolstoy,
writing poetry,
picturing you in wire-rimmed glasses and faded jeans
playing guitar
still caught in the Revolution
of the sixties.
Out of love, comrade,
woman like myself in art and consciousness, sister
in whose notes rise and lower
inherently, my hope.

The Smells I Remember In the House
Of My First Lover

Pot,
Peanut Butter,
Vanilla Musk.
Incense….
Burning logs,
Smouldering logs
coffee.

Reincarnation

I come to myself staring   a plain
goblet of wine in my hand   holding
me here
a lighted candle,
incense burning
a velvet chair
a ticking clock

A world of dim and evil light.
I live. I die. I am born again.
Everything will remain the same
It doesn't matter
a lighted candle,
incense burning
a velvet chair
a ticking clock.

I come to myself   a black
cat on the chair beside me   holding
me here   earthbound
until I am born again.

Reincarnation II

I am sitting in my velvet chair
reading a first issue
of an old Life Magazine
The great wings of the fan spread
the air around me, my cat
looks at the air and meows
He sees something
he leaps from the arm of the chair.
Rain continues to pound outside
I get up to put another log in the fire
and notice
the shadow of a woman who has been here
before
resting on the window.

Adam Baum Eggs

chickens drop them
into the nests below

Eastern Poem

My lover went out to buy Chinese food, late getting back,
　　　3 AM and she still isn't here;
though they don't let on, my Italian parents worry
　　　that I must be starving.
They don't know I'm by my eastern window
　　　fiddling with a pen and rice paper
and my lover's in the middle of the river
　　　in a boat competing with Li Po
over who can write the best vegetable poem.

Invitation To Breakfast

I want to melt like hot butter under your knife
tonight, so
tomorrow you can spread me on your toast
along with the strawberry jam
This is an invitation to choose among fruits
ripening in my garden
and there's no limit to the number of helpings.

Getting Ready
For A Poetry Reading
   (after Michael Lassell)

The poems will have been written by a lesbian
with a love of sestinas and sonnets.
Sit alone in the second aisle directly in front
of the poet. Make eye contact.
A Marxist will sit next to you.
"It's cold outside," he will say.
You will wonder if he walked.
Don't ask. Focus instead on the poet's short cropped hair.
She will hope you think she is
a Marxist too, but don't be
deceived.

The room becomes crowded. Your mind starts to wander
Will she look like she sounds?
Will she be militant?
Will she be timid?

Think of the following things:
      the pain in your shoulders
      last week when you
      carried three cords of wood
      into the shed;

      the finger you broke
      two weeks ago
      playing softball;

      the tightness of your bra
      as it tries unsuccessfully
      to hold up
      your sagging breasts.

Fear the most:
      your headache is a symptom of a brain tumor
      (Wonder if your insurance will cover.)
      know that you need to see
      your doctor. Demand a cat scan.
      Demand socialization of medicine.
      Wonder how to pay for it with poetry.

Try to get your mind off your headache:
      desire the woman sitting in the third row;
      laugh whenever the poet says anything remotely
      funny;
      applaud loudly after her coming out poem.

When you leave the reading, there will be a mad rush
        for the exits.
        Everyone will run to their Volkswagens.

Give every driver the finger. Become assertive.

Arrive home exhausted. Eat cold pizza.
Stare at the autographed poet's book.
Sit on the sofa staring at it
Until dawn.

It will be the fifth anniversary of your first publication,
a tiny poem in an obscure magazine, but
you will tell
no one. You will
drive to NYC and photograph the gay parade.
You will applaud jill johnston, the radical
you saw at NYU on tuesday, and you will
weep over the rejection
of the ERA.

You will vow to drive a Volkswagen always. To hate
Phyllis Schlafly. You will fear the lack of spiritualism
in America. You will fear America's greed.

The next day you will
go to another reading,
experience yet more humiliation
of the flesh, fear for the future,
experience more pain,

and write another poem.

Blocked Writer
  (after Terry Stokes)

& now I am so worried I cannot
write a line without thinking
am I fucking it up?

& this is only the title,
& I've taken every writing course
& I've listened to every poet writing in America
& I've memorized all of Grimm & I'm right

back where I began, in my mother's womb,
banging, weeping, wiggling my little
finger, searching for a key.

Corporation

I have spent my life
climbing beanstalks
Only to find greedy giants
at the top.

In Moderation
    (after Frank O'Hara)

I am a woman of few excesses.
I am cautious who I talk to.
I buy cheap jeans that I let fade.
I eat small steaks.

But sometimes it's so great when I
get out of bed late
and drink too much Scotch
and smoke too much pot
and love you too much.

Black Friday
(a parody of Diane Wakoski's "Blue Monday")

You are dead: wound round like a curled up
                    black cat.
I cannot shake you out of my black satin sheets.
                    Your name
is still wedged in every corner of my waterbed.

Death passed me in a black mortician suit.
His glass cane, hollow and filled with
skeleton heads and bones...
He wore black patent leather shoes
His mustache was black and waxy.

"Death," I said.
"I beg your pardon," he said.
"Mr. Death," I said.
"I beg your pardon," he said.

So I saw there was no use bothering him on
                    the street.

Death passed me on the street in a black
mortician suit. He knew you already.
I could tell.

Incense And Poetry
(to Diane DiPrima)

Like the Kalliope Wheel
The full moon
looms over us
The white smoke spirals up
from the silver incense holder
And perfumes the quiet room

You say you are inspired
by Tibetans, Alchemists, Taoists
You sign my book
Happy May Eve

The wind
carries the notes of your song
to our ears
And who, other than a poet
would wear a necklace of heads?

Jill's Fairy Tale

tonight my MOTHER fell over the wall and cracked
the confused wax wings of the alarm CLOCK
                turned toward the sun
and melted in their lust for power
what would we do without THEM!
i fell through a hole
alice told me to get lost
                to find another hole
all the squinty-eyed queens protested
a kid put his wax finger in a dyke to prevent flooding.
she nearly killed him while blanketing
                the idea that none could swim.
my belly soaked up the juices of an indigestible rabbit
when i stayed for dinner
alice protested
the queen offered herself as dessert
all the king's horses and men stayed home and wept
all the women advanced united carrying lifeboats
"we can swim but we don't want to"
"the rabbit died" said the cheshire cat "i wanted him"
then he led the crooked army of men bearing real guns
"there wouldn't be wars if it was up to us" i raved
they told me to get out of everybody's tales
so i took the fur foot
and lewis wished me better luck next time.

January 29th, 1987

(year of the cat—CHINESE ASTROLOGY
Jan 29th 1987-Feb 16th 1988)

Cat bones in the tree
the fire department never came.

The Fury of Gretel
   (after Anne Sexton)

The breadcrumbs lie
in a row
along the path
Brown, white, all
scattered through the
                forest.
Remember, Hansel, when you laughed at me
for not being able to tie
my own shoe
or
cut my own meat
or get away from
a spanking?
You even made me give up
my belief in Santa Claus.
Remember, big brother,
when you knew I couldn't swim
but threw me
in the pool anyway?
The world wasn't
mine.
It belonged to you
and the big people.
Over my bed
you stood in a wolf costume
one night
and made shadows over my head.
But remember I'm the one
who saved you this time
by pushing the witch
into the oven.
Leaving breadcrumbs was a
really stupid idea.
Oh Brother
I want to get home
it is dark,
where are the big people,
when will I get there,
taking small steps
behind you
all day
each day
and finally making it
alone.

Poem To Confessional Poets
    (to Anne Sexton and Sylvia Plath)

In my flyers cap
I tiptoe across the sea
dreaming of you high in the mountains
gathering fog
and singing about the death you love.
Next to really terrible things
my life seems more steady.
Like a stone below a raging fire
I know I will endure.

Anticipation

Hidden in his studio apartment
Rumpelstiltskin masturbates
High in her tower,
The princess sits and waits
reading Russian novels
about snow
to beat off
the heat.

Lying on my hotel bed
reading Grimm
I fantasize about us
in Provincetown last summer
lying on the coarse sand
facing the parted dunes
wondering if you came
this year
wondering if you'll remember
my name.

I Have Seen A Woman
Reading Alone In Her Chair

I have seen
a woman sitting
between the stove
and the Star Sirius
butting a Camel cigarette
in a cat food can
I have seen
a woman eating
tiny hollow robin bones
sipping Miller High Life Beer.
I have seen
a woman screaming through lace curtains
at the Milky Way
I have seen

Dear Writer,

        We regret that the manuscript
  does not meet the needs
             of the magazine
at this time. You see,
          even though your poems
  show suffering and knowledge
             of the ass of the devil,
      the edge of death and madness
             rejection by men and women
      the weirdness of advertising   the magic of
          astrology and love
            confrontation with the muses ass,
and the knowledge of the cosmos,
        We reget to say
  that you have just not starved, gambled, and died
               enough.
Please try us again
      after you've risked some REAL danger,
Until then SUFFER, SUFFER, SUFFER.

            Regretfully,

            The Editors

Sitting Reading William Carlos Williams

Yes I can still hear you William
begging forgiveness in the night.
Sitting turning my page I too
am thinking about your last two
plums in the refrigerator.
Please forgive me for having eaten them
but I was hungry and
all that was left was an old drumstick
a pickle
a solitary penumbra
and those plums
so sweet and so cold.

Hiking Next To Mt. St. Helens
(after Gary Snyder)

coming
watching
a volcano

Woman

This life is like no other.
The rye bread rising in the oven.
The almond coffee brewing.
Walking with you under dark pines,
a collection of one hundred short
poems on love in your hand.

Restless Night
    (to Anne Sexton)

The night passes.
Anne sleeps beside me.
"She is a woman," I whisper to myself.
"She is not part of these dreams you are always having."
She moves closer to me in the darkness.
I look up from my bed
into the kitchen and see a muse dead
asleep on the stove.

Postpartum Blues
    (to Janis Joplin)

It was a cold day to die in.
Cats cried behind bare trees.
I raised greens
and patterned the world with my stick
I tried to measure the sky
while poking words into neat lines.
Janis lifted blues
through her eternal soul
By way of New York and Los Angeles.
Her hands clapped more passion
than all the clackling beads
that have ever been muttered on by cats in black
Her hoarse voice screeched more pain
than any stupefied singer's lungs
could summon from fretful notes.
Death was the design and song she entered.

The Poem That I Will Be Remembered For

My best poem will have ocean
right in the middle of it, ocean so cold and deep
with life my friend will leave behind
his scuba outfit and tell me, "Wear this when you
go in." My best poem
will have night in it, too, and all the stars
in the Eastern sky; and this immense body
of water shining for miles under a new moon.
My best poem will have a jacuzzi
and a shower for itself, skylights,
a phone by the faucet,
a soapdish made from a clam shell
picked from the beach an hour before breakfast.
There'll be waves breaking in my best poem;
and a beach where ocean-soaked
shellfish will rise up, consuming one another.
Oh, my best poem will throw tides!
But there won't be any waterglasses in my best poem.
I'll take up drinking from the bottle.

Poem To Freshman
  (after Blaise Cendrars)

We are sorry to announce your
Anthropology 101 class has been cancelled.
Your professor has been eaten by cannibals
in the Amazon
The Meteorological Institute announces hurricanes
from here on in
the ozone layer is completely gone
And finally we wish to announce that your future is
in great jeopardy.

Waking Up Gay
In Upstate, New York

No forest hues for now
for now no sexual rites
just Sanka in the morning
Beethoven, and breakfast stares.

Floorwalkers

Don't sell shoes
Sell dreams
of ruby slippers
and lovers on dragons
riding naked toward the sun.
At night, I
alone in my one room apartment,
play Vivaldi
on my stereo
wondering
if all Judy's are really
dead, or just living
in Kansas.

Healing Powers

Soup and
a good book
Edgar Cayce
chicken noodle
a tune
called The Dark Side of the Moon
Rooms open themselves
open their doors their windows
light their blue lights
it can only get better.

Astral Projection

Now that I notice it is my body which has been
    drifting back and forth above the clouds
        drifting amongst the sparrows
            over the plastic pink flamingos
                on the neighbors' lawn
                    over the highways
                        of the galaxies
                            through the great door
                                towards heaven
                                    toward you.

Toto, I Don't Think We're In
    Kansas Anymore

We should have known
Days before, the big rain
the shifting wind, the near dry land

You remind me of Judy
singing "Somewhere Over the Rainbow…"

We got caught up in it
instead of finding Oz
we found our feet sticking out from under
the house that felled us.

The season of tornados is here: even
the forest trees snicker obscenities.

Movies are our only escape—I think of poor Toto
trapped under your arm.

Face it we can't win the lottery
and wizardry isn't all
it's cracked up to be.

Toto, I Don't Think We're In Kansas
          Anymore Part II

          astral projection or out-of-body travel
          is described as the projection, or externalization,
          of the astral body from the physical body.

And then I lift a luminous
ruby shoe from your foot.
We talk,
stare into the fire,
become irrelevant.

I go out quietly
arriving anywhere in three minutes.
The trick is if a train or a plane comes
there is only room for the sea.

Facing East

I smell baked chestnuts
on the woodstove
as I lie naked
on my oriental rug
reading Kabir.

Are You Warm Enough Or Shall I
Put Another Log In The Fire?

I drink fine wine
          and
          I drink some more.

                    I eat lobster by candlelight
                         or steak
                    whichever I choose.

I prefer a life
with choices.

                    Once I drank enough cheap rum
                         to kill Socrates.

and I ate enough breadcrumbs
to make Hansel jealous,

                              and I lost you.

But then again in those times,
I had no other choice.

Illusionists

I don't know why MAGIC
means so much to me
The answer lies
somewhere in my subconscious I suppose.
A world in which my drawers contain a hundred
wands, tarot cards, a rabbit's foot.

Perhaps it's the enchantment of the Word
abracadabra or the feel of
the furry white ears between my fist.

Trolls, Witches, and Trains

Between Anne Sexton's TRANSFORMATIONS and the train station
is no easy journey. Rumpelstiltskin with Truman's asexual voice
is in my mind. I envision now so many faces: Snow White
with eyes wide as Orphan Annie, a wolf dressed in frills
like a transvestite, a maid who looked like Al Jolson,
the conductor who stared at me when I dropped my book
to give him my ticket, a kid who looked like a dwarf as
he ran up the aisle, an old woman with four whiskers
under her lip and brown spots on her hand
who smiled at me as she walked by.
I never thought of Rapunzel as a lesbian
until now. Anne
I have truly been transformed on the Amtrak
between Upstate, New York and New York City.

The Disappearance Of WT Grant Stores

The gerbils in the bargain basement
nolonger run around in their squeaky wheels
The turtles below the plastic palm trees
nolonger struggle on their backs
The fluorescent lights along the food counter
nolonger light
The balloons nolonger pop
promising you 50 cents off a banana split
the smell of polyester, cotton, and
stale popcorn nolonger exists
since the WT GRANT stores disappeared.

A News First

In 1974 in Sarasota, Florida, a local television personality named Chris Chuback shot herself in the head while announcing the news. She said "In keeping with Channel 40's policy of having the news first, you are going to see another first--an attempted suicide." The station blacked out and switched to temporary programming.

The stations when they black out
when they turn to something more conventional, move on
drawing sunlight out of the air.
Somewhere in a studio in space—in a green room
she rummages in her purse
for a gun and moves it in her slim tailored skirt
to play a trick on herself.
So clean, lipsticked, dressed with microphone
in shirt, she sits spaced out.
But to watch it. She announces between the news
of Willie's homerun and rain prediction—an attempt at suicide.
In many places and now in hundreds of places
from her death, they hear it and wonder if it's real as
her eyeballs roll in her struggle to rise
above the towers of man,   to dream of fame
above the beds of past lovers,   who put her down
above the other personalities,   who will wake
to see the woman they should be—struggling on rooftops
to become stars.

Who'd You Think You Were Anyways?

Ahead of you is the day
with its ball of thread.
Behind you is the unattainable dream
of success.
You shot for the sky
thinking you were Superwoman
in your superficial briefs.
More than a housewife? Ha!
You pissed in the sink
when faucets drove
like storms on white porcelain.
Spatula in hand
padding down the room, you turn around
to see a woman
with stones in her hands predicting only more rain.

Poem To Gertrude And Alice

While I was eating hash brownies
the other night
I thought of you
It was 3 AM on the floor mattress
incense burning
20's music on the stereo
Dori in my arms
watching the stars
"It must have been great
to have hung out with poets
and artists and bohemians
back then," she said.
I agreed
The moon loomed over
the skylight
She handed me another
hash brownie.

Hemingway's Cats

Ernest how did you do it
write I mean
with all of those cats around you?
All the photos I see of you
in Key West show your
stout figure at your desk
a black cat atop your lap
an orange one upon the window sill.
As I write this
my cat paws at my pen
nibbles at its tip
as if writing a poem
weren't hard enough
without this furry distraction.
Ernest how did you do it
write I mean?

Poem To An Adulterous Spouse

Tonight you are eating Hansel and Gretel's breadcrumbs
and I am making a drink that could kill Socrates.
You are wearing your Moby Dick
printed cotton pajamas, and I am wearing my skin
turned inside out.
I can smell in your hair the cedar
of the motel bedroom
and I want to say
that tonight only your hands can warm my anger.

Poem To Li Po
And All The Guys
Down At The Yellow River

Sitting on my futon
eating tofu
staring at the bookshelves
filled with Chinese haiku,
I am meditating to subdue
the evil dragon.

Reeking of patchouli incense,
my dog Tu Fu is asleep
at the foot of my futon
belly up
I am contemplating,
attaining Nirvana.

Wonderland

At the tea party, in that rouge of light
of ten or eleven mushrooms, you could pass
for the white rabbit; we could hop all night
in and out of holes and through looking glass
in flying, shining Nikes. As Alice
my body grows much larger as we dine,
your white tail bops nervously through a kiss.
I grow intelligent about the wine.
But this high life is trying; cheshire cats
take us from the table, hand in white paw
we seek more thrills—a mad man in a hat,
caterpillars, and crazy queens with saws.
In this land I'd rather stay in my hole
than risk the chance of losing my white soul.

Voyeur

At Café de la Paix
women walk by braless
men slide by. I must say I prefer
the white wine over the red.
My friend says, "Let's go to the Catmandu."
Her eyes wander as the wine ticks
in her head.
A cat rubs against my bare leg
I prefer life in slow motion
the sun in my face
my senses filled with perfume
only advancing as far as the expresso.

Sitting By My Bullard Woodstove

Sitting by my Bullard* woodstove
a log burning gently,
warmth coming over me
in my 'Whales Save Us' tee shirt
heart underpants
gray wool sox
stroking my huge black cat, I
think about the Aurora Borealis
the Dog Star Sirius
and you—
not necessarily in that order.

*Bullard brand woodstoves had a huge
  gold eagle on the front of them.

Well-Endowed, Affectionate Writer
German Shepard Puppy
Seeks Female
Shepard For *Hassle-Free Sex*.

I stand 2 feet tall and have a
big 12" tail. I'm just waiting to
help break-up you and your mate.
I'll do anything...I don't care.
You can be my master
then I'll be yours. Make me
obey your commands...train me.
Tie me to a leash and then
take me for a walk dressed in
doll clothes. What the hell...
I'll play-out your fantasies...
suck on you tail in front of
your friends...
degrade you while your mate
watches...woof! I'll even go on
your rug! How about that?
If you're a female shepard
we can met on Wescott Street
and play cat + mouse in
our nice cars. If you think
you're the type that can handle
discreet encounters in alleys,
backyards or the bushes,
please write me and enclose
a super-revealing photo:
Box K-9, New York Times.
PURINA-COLADA LOVERS NEED
NOT REPLY.

Waking Up in Upstate, New York
With Someone I'm Afraid To Love
Because You Hurt Me So Badly

"And so the world
chilled, and the women wept, tore at their hair.
Yet, in the skies, a goddess governed Sirius, the Dog,
Who shines alike on mothers, lesbians, and whores."

                    --A PASTICHE FOR EVE
                    Weldon Kees

    Wake me gently
    from the first cold sheets
    of November,
    when logs have been smouldering
    half the night while we were
    making love
    and thinking about that Dogon Star Sirius
    57,000,000,000,000 miles away.

The Ten Virtues Of Incense Burning

Incense burning opens the mind to divinity.
Incense burning cleanses the mind.
Incense burning divests the mind of worldly impurities.
Incense burning wakes up the mind.
Incense burning encourages the mind in solitude.
Incense burning affords the mind peace when it is busy.
One cannot burn too much incense.
Yet, even a little incense is enough.
Age does not affect the efficacy of incense.
Habitual use of incense causes no harm.

After Reading Cinderella
One Quiet Sunday Afternoon
In A Gay Men's Bar I
Have A Startling Revelation

There are no ugly old queens left—
They have all been murdered
in the pages
of fairytales.

Adventure

Gretel puts on her
LL Bean down vest
and TIMBERLAND hiking boots
and hitchhikes
down the pathways—
her knapsack stuffed with dreams.

The Virtues Of Having
Cats As Pets

1. They don't argue.

2. They don't ask for money.

3. They don't stay out
   until 2AM, then lie to
   you about where they've been.

4. They sleep with you
   no matter what.

5. They listen to Vivaldi.

6. They don't talk in their sleep.

7. They let you write poems about them
   without explanation.

The Zen Of Writing Poetry

My muse sits naked
at her typewriter
in a temple courtyard
near L.A.
I sit at my wordprocessor
in Upstate, NY
We are and are not together.

Nuclear War

Enjoy the morning
rising late in the East
baking bread
Enjoy reading the NY Times
before a roaring fire
Enjoy watching the sunset
drinking expensive wine
listening to Mahler
Then make yourself a sandwich
of rye bread, & provolone cheese
lots of it
& drink After the Fall Apple Juice
& sit down
& write a poem
while you still can.

Printed in the United States
By Bookmasters